Chasing Time

Meiko Barnard

BookLeaf Publishing

India | USA | UK

Presentation by *BookLeaf Publishing*

Web: www.bookleafpub.com

E-mail: info@bookleafpub.com

ISBN: 9789363302952

First edition 2024

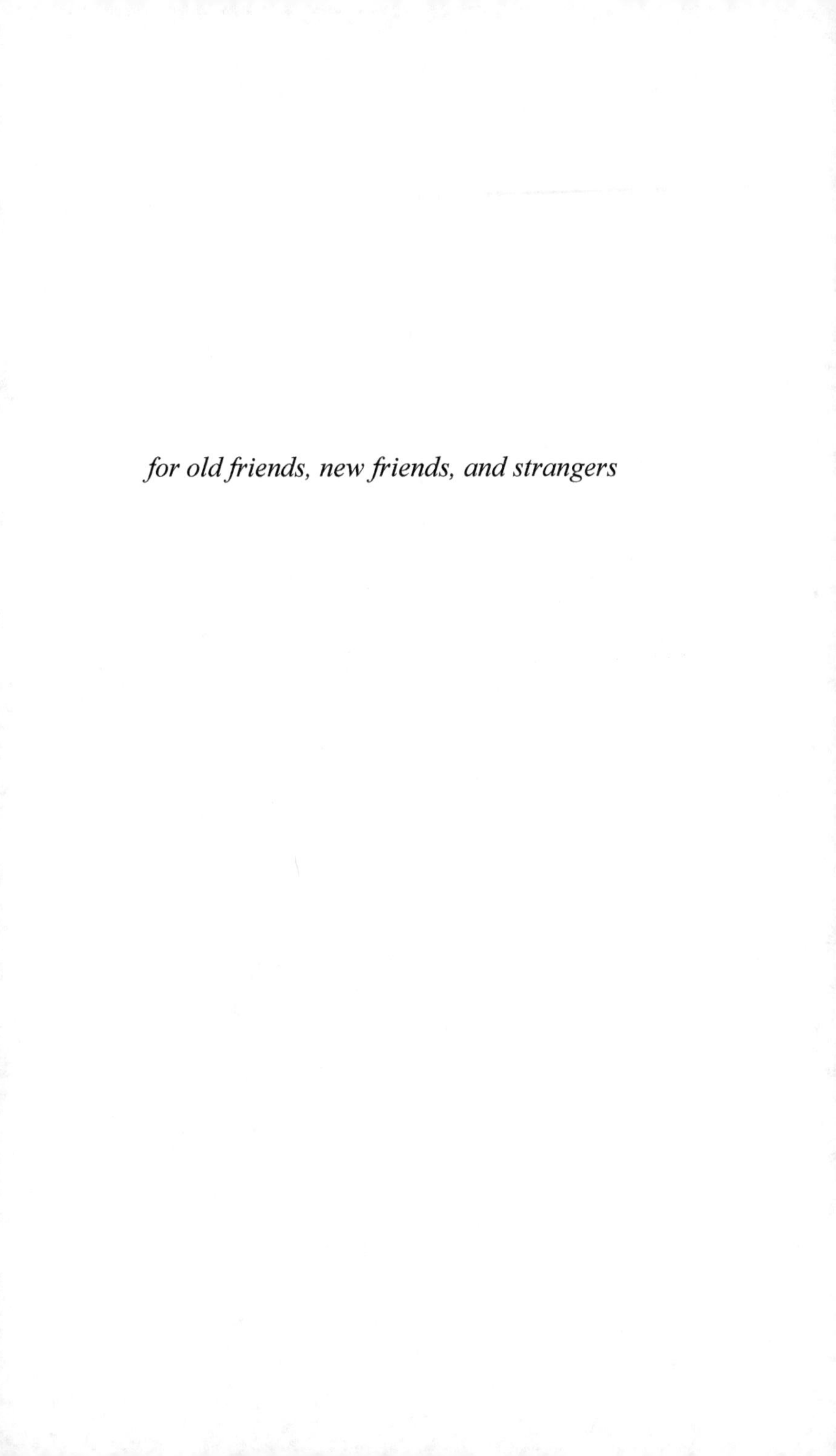

for old friends, new friends, and strangers

ACKNOWLEDGEMENT

One year ago today, I did not think I would be writing a book, much less publishing one. I would like to extend a massive thank you to Bookleaf Publishing for this wonderful opportunity!

This collection of poetry would never have been written if not for each and every one of the people in my life. I would like to take a moment to appreciate all of those friends who have come and gone and all of those friends who have stayed.

Finally, I would like to express my gratitude for my family, who have been steadfast through all of life's changes.

PREFACE

Writing this collection was a journey through nostalgia and an exploration of expectations. Society often pressures us to maintain friendships indefinitely, but true value lies in those who return, time and again, despite life's silences and constant changes. This book is a tribute to those enduring connections that make us who we are.

mud pies

sometimes,
i like to sit and watch
time tick by like a broken clock
sometimes,
i like to lie down and wonder:
why is my ceiling painted blue?

occasionally,
a little bug will wander
across my outstretched pinky finger
occasionally the bug when held will stay
but if i leave for long he always flies away.

perhaps one day,
i'll find a gentle ladybug
whose spots are red and black
(nothing in between)
and perhaps one day she'll join my
picnic tea party

and we can eat mud pies
and be little girls again.

sometimes,
i wonder why

we stopped - we'd built
a kingdom of sandcastles
high in the sky,
sometimes,
i wonder if our sandcastles eroded
just as our swingset-calloused hands have.

occasionally,
when i think about all that time
flying with the beetles, arms
looped around rusted chains,
i wonder:
whatever happened to Yesterday?

midnight charades

we whiled away Yesterday
with a game of midnight charades
in the wild carefree thrill of night
we forgot how we
were the butterfly and bee and me.

perhaps it was that in the dark
the light of day seemed to
f
a
l
l

                    a w a y

                              we threw on an

old pink scarf;

                              you were the

Princess,

                              and I the

Knight of Beetles,

and running
back

                              and forth,

across the room

through the words we couldn't say,

                                        giddy,

under the ceiling, under the stars,

it almost seemed

like everything would be okay.

.

.

.

                          but midnight charades

is just

                              a game we

played

                                    Yesterday

                          and today the morning

light is bright

                        and we threw aside the

pink scarf

                            and i can't help

but feel

                                    that we're

d   r   i   f   t   i
n   g

5

apart.

yesterday, we were new friends

we were just two people who saw each other
just once was all it took
and then we were two people who loved each
other.

it was never the sort of love that meant
quiet kisses in the dark
it was the sort of love that meant
midnight charades and popsicles and mud pies
the sort of love that was measured in tears
and years, and whispered confessions of our
greatest fears.

i wore the pink scarf like a crown, and you
passed me the tea. we laughed as it spilled
over red-checkered blanket and grass warmed by
the sun.

we were two people who thought that Someday
would never come, and we never said goodbye
because the one fear that neither of us dared
confess
was that Someday would come
and we might say goodbye.

who made right triangles in the stars

we waltzed there, swaying softly
caught in a dream: inky caress of darkness
and stage of mildewed leaves. i said,
i think somewhere here in the midnight
is where i'd like to stay. you said,
wouldn't it be nice, to forever evade Tomorrow?

a pirouette or two or three, and dizzy, we
collapse
onto the muddy dewy ground, where you point
up
and your fingers trace the stars, and your
shoulder brushes mine
in agreement with the silence, time only an
afterthought,
for a minute or a lifetime we smile and make
right triangles of distant suns.

i think how easy it would be, to lose
myself to this dream. to lose what i could never
be, to lose
what i thought i'd be. for a long time we could
pretend

that Tomorrow doesn't loom past coming hour,
and that
Yesterday doesn't follow each fleeting stolen
moment,
and that there is no string of words hanging taut
between us.

for a long time,
we made right triangles of the stars.

but i guess we're strangers
now

there grew a dissonance between us,
a terrible twisting thing:
it started with a space after goodbye.

one day will pass. i'll linger over
the kind of popsicle that tastes like childhood
and blue dye on my fingertips
will make me think of you.

two days and three days
i'll wonder if that space after goodbye
means we both need space to grow apart.

next it'll be three days
four
Yesterday slips into Tomorrow
time's orchestration ensures that
Someday will come without you.

and before i know,
it'll be a month

six months

Monday will make it one year ago today
that there came a space after goodbye.
for a moment, i'll wonder: should i still
be missing you? and,
am i allowed to grieve?

when the only life you've faded from is mine.

saudade

you hold it in your hand, a delicate
fluttering thing; an awfully fragile, desperate
thing. it has dust-soft wings, paper thin and
frayed
at the edges like the childhood art piece
swept under my bed that once
i thought was the most important thing in the
world.

it has little antennae, and one might be missing,
calling back to the cat with the missing ear
that used to sit on the fence outside
and watch our picnics and watch as you and I
promised over apple slices that we would never
change.

it's just a tiny, struggling thing, and you begin to
fear
that if you open your hand and let it go, it might
fly straight into the flame -- you might have to
watch
as its wings are eaten by fire, and its wet eyes
turn gray and dry
and then, with stone feet, you might have to bury
it with all those things

that rest beneath the tombstones in your mind.

so you hold it, hating that you hope its ceaseless
scrabble
against your palm never relents
and you wonder,
if it's worth saving this life.

i still wonder

are we strangers now
(or were we strangers then)
and why are we strangers now
(and why were we strangers then)

maybe it's the way we stopped
to pose for pictures - glass eyes
and painted smiles, glowing
pixels in a time capsule

the pictures stayed the same
frozen laughter, one year ago today
but we all spun apart; you
in your world, and i in mine

am i still meant to prise your face
from mass of milling crowd

or will the nameless mob consume

our laughter and
our memories?

when, in passing, we speak
will it be of who we were, one

year ago today, or will you say

sorry,
polite smile on your lips,
i didn't mean to brush your shoulder.

and
i just want to know
are we strangers now,
or were we strangers then
(one year ago today)
and why are we strangers now?

and how could we be strangers now.

little girls again

i find myself kept up at night
staring at the ceiling, discordant
music and empty space
captivated by dreaming
of future summers
just like that one:

we played charades every night,
the beetle and the ladybug and me
our games pushed sunrise; we never
seemed to lose the pink scarf

i passed it to the ladybug and she
wrapped it around me
and i shared with the beetle
i didn't know i was covering his wings;

i hoped that time would never end
what would have happened if it hadn't?
to the beetle and the ladybug and me.

but now the pink scarf lays flat
in the empty space.

are memories like fossils?

and will they crumble, like
65 million years just did
a limestone oyster,
held to the wavering sunlight

it feels like sacrilege
shattered stone dusting my fingertips
a hundred thousand lifetimes f
                    l
      u
                t
t
   e
r
        i
n

   g

down, down, down
to capture the sunlight one last time
golden dusk highlighted
by the corpse of Yesterday.

and if all those stone memories
can crumble in my soft hands
what's to stop the future
the Someday, the impending Tomorrow
from cracking under the weight
of all the terrible broken bones of Yesterday?

i thought about saying sorry

Yesterday i went to speak with you,

my racing heart pled, just make it through
and in my visceral fairytale you said

"I'm sorry too."

space

it's time to let time be

and see

that Yesterday, we saw each other

so that the you and i

of Someday

would know what to look for.

chasing time

so much time spent chasing time

and only because i was afraid:
if you stopped seeing me, would i become
invisible?
but we spoke last week, and even though your
voice has changed
that space after goodbye seems a little warmer
and one year ago today looks like old friends,
not
strangers (because we could never be strangers).

so much time spent chasing time

tugging at the coattails of Someday while
clinging
with clammy palms to Yesterday's loose fingers
because i made Tomorrow a stranger, and i
clung so hard to the lives i was losing
i forgot about the life i had left.

old friends

we don't talk every day like we used to
there are no new pictures of you after
one year ago today. but you left
your pink scarf at my house
and your words in my head.

our shoulders will brush on the street
next week. you'll laugh and say hello,
it's nice to see you, and we'll talk about

all the things that changed
(your voice, your hair
that smile when you talk
about your new coworker
and the purple scarf sticking
out of your sweater)

and all the things
that never could change
(these little conversations
and the times we used to have.
a certain particular curve of your lips,
and the color of your eyes)

we don't talk every day
but we'll always be old friends.

what i thought was goodbye

turned out to be a slow settling
of all that you were to me
into all the spaces that i never knew what to do
with.

the time we spent together crept
into all those cracks and gaps
and in this way, old friends are never lost.

and now as time goes by

i find you in the liminal space
at the edge of sleep
and in the quiet pauses of the day

i hear your laughter
beneath the branches of the trees
we used to climb

our paths diverged
and your shadow no longer follows mine
when i wade through tall grass
to lay down the old picnic blanket.

it used to feel like grief
but now it just feels like change
the same change as day and night
and high tide to low tide.

retrospect

i used to think that someday

i wouldn't see your face and search my mind
for a thousand ways to fix us; Someday

i wouldn't fear memory's sleight of hand
when i walked into Tomorrow; Someday

i wouldn't wonder: what

did i do wrong

to lose you all

to lose myself.

Someday, i would not frantically stare
at one year ago today; Someday,

i would kick my legs up and fly,
serenaded by the squeak of rust,
and i would close my eyes and
think of midnight,
and i would smile behind the pink scarf,

and Someday,
i would vanquish Yesterday.

speaking of someday

wrapped round my wrist, a scarlet string
a bracelet whose silver letters can't say what life
will bring

once i thought i knew what those letters spelled
but now i think: is it so artless? to crave the
wicked kiss
of cold lips of deliverance atop that softest skin?

is it so desperate? to fiddle with a knot of twine,
and feel duty fall unbound from forearm to floor,

to glory in freedom whilst craving something
more;
is it so hopeless? this wish of mine to know now
or never know what those silver letters spell.

all that you mean to me

i. i saw what the world could be.

remembering when i found you:
shiny dime, newly minted penny feelings
silver tongue, wild spirit.
love, in a plastic box.

ii. and in your same soul,

remembering when i lost you:
when desperation in the dark
could never be enough.
you pleaded: help me!
but i never heard you.

iii. i found hope

remembering your goodbye:
resignation, then acceptance
how we never knew
that we were hurting each other
when it came time to let go.

iv. that Someday we'd be free.

two years ago today

you and i thought the world would end
because the royal "we" was clunky off
our tongues and because you and i
thought that goodbye was all there could be.

but that's two years ago, today
and the world didn't end
you and i are our own people
and i still call you friend.

soon it'll be ten years ago, today
we'll laugh over two years ago, today
still neither of us will know what those
silver letters spell; but i think we'll come to see
that you and i grew into something better.

in another life

the butterfly and bee and me
would never have flown apart
and in another life,
you and i would be a royal we.

we'll never know if that other life
(where we would be strangers to you and i)
would be the life we dreamed of
at midnight every night.

but i am so happy
to know the you of this life.

in this life

i will love you a little more
every time i think of mud pies
and midnight charades
and being little girls.

in this life
i'm glad we're old friends.